The Virtual You:

"Creating a Memorable Online Presence and Building your Brand"

Christiana John

Copyright © 2023 by [Christiana John]

All rights reserved. No part of this book may be reproduced, scanned, or distributed in any printed or electronic form without permission.

This publication is protected by copyright law and is intended for the personal use of the reader. No part of this publication may be sold, shared, or used for commercial purposes without the express permission of the author.

Contents

Chapter 1 5

Introduction 5

    Overview of personal growth and development 6

    Importance of building a personal online presence 8

Chapter 2 11

    Defining Your Personal Brand 11

    The importance of defining your personal brand 12

    Understanding your values, strengths, and unique qualities 14

    Creating a personal mission statement 17

Chapter 3 23

Building a personal online presence 23

    Understanding the role of social media in personal branding 24

    Choosing the right social media platforms for your personal brand .25

    Developing a strong online presence through content creation 28

    Optimizing your online profiles for search engines 30

Chapter 4 33

Networking and building relationships 33

    The power of networking in personal branding 34

    Building relationships through social media 36

    Developing strong communication skills 38

Chapter 5 40

Balancing authenticity and adaptability 40

    Balancing Authenticity with Adaptability 42

    Importance of being authentic in personal branding 43

    Navigating different online and in-person environments 44

Conclusion 46

Chapter 1

Introduction

In the digital age, personal growth and self-development are becoming increasingly important aspects of our lives. Building a personal online presence and leveraging social media can greatly enhance one's personal growth journey. With the rise of digital technology, the internet has become a powerful tool for self-expression, learning, and networking, making it easier for individuals to build a personal online presence that can help boost their careers and personal brands. A strong personal online presence can help individuals showcase their skills, passions, and perspectives while also creating opportunities for growth and self-discovery. In this age of digital connectivity, it's more important than ever to understand how to build and maintain a positive and impactful personal online presence. This includes understanding the basics of social media, the role it plays in personal growth, and the strategies for leveraging it for personal development. Whether you are looking to build your personal brand, network with like-minded individuals, or simply share your ideas with the world, this book is an essential resource for anyone who is committed to personal growth and self-development in the digital age.

Overview of personal growth and development

Personal growth and self-development are two interconnected concepts that are crucial for a fulfilling and satisfying life. Personal growth refers to the process of improving one's character, abilities, and overall quality of life, while self-development involves acquiring new knowledge, skills, and experiences to achieve personal growth. Both concepts are lifelong journeys that require dedication, commitment, and a willingness to continuously learn and grow.

Personal growth and self-development can encompass a wide range of areas, including mental, emotional, physical, and spiritual aspects of life. For example, someone may choose to focus on improving their mental well-being by practicing mindfulness or meditation, while another person may choose to develop their physical health by taking up regular exercise. The goal of personal growth and self-development is to live a more fulfilling and meaningful life by becoming the best version of oneself.

Self-development can be achieved through a variety of means, such as reading books, attending workshops and seminars, or taking courses in areas of interest. Personal growth can also be facilitated through therapy, mentorship, or personal coaching. It is important to find a balance between personal growth and self-development that works for each individual and to tailor one's journey to their unique needs and goals.

One of the benefits of personal growth and self-development is increased self-awareness. When we become more aware of our thoughts, emotions, and behaviors, we can make more informed decisions about how to improve our lives. For example, someone who is struggling with anxiety may choose to focus on developing their mindfulness and stress-management skills, which can lead to a reduction in anxiety and an improvement in overall well-being.

In addition to improving our mental and emotional well-being, personal growth and self-development can also help us to build better relationships. When we are more self-aware and better equipped to handle our emotions, we are better able to communicate effectively and build meaningful connections with others. Furthermore, by developing our skills and knowledge, we can contribute more effectively to society and make a positive impact on the world.

Personal growth and self-development are lifelong journeys that require effort and dedication. However, the rewards of a fulfilling and meaningful life make the effort well worth it. Whether it's through reading, learning, or engaging in personal growth activities, it's important to take time for self-reflection and to continually strive for self-improvement.

In conclusion, personal growth and self-development are crucial aspects of a fulfilling and meaningful life. By continuously working to improve oneself, one can live a more self-aware and purposeful life, build better relationships, and make a positive impact in the world. By dedicating time and effort to personal growth and self-development, individuals can achieve their full potential and live their best lives.

Importance of building a personal online presence

Building a personal online presence has become increasingly important in today's digital age. Having a strong online presence can help you achieve your personal and professional goals, increase your visibility, and enhance your reputation. Whether you're an entrepreneur, a job seeker, or simply looking to build a personal brand, having a well-crafted online presence can be incredibly beneficial.

One of the most important reasons for building a personal online presence is to increase your visibility and reach a larger audience. Social media platforms, such as Facebook, Twitter, and LinkedIn, allow you to connect with millions of people around the world. By sharing your thoughts, ideas, and experiences, you can engage with others, form new relationships, and increase your exposure. This can be particularly valuable if you're looking to build your brand or grow your business, as it gives you access to a wider audience than you might otherwise have.

Having a personal online presence also allows you to present yourself in the best possible light. You can showcase your skills, experiences, and achievements, and share your personality and values with others. This can help you build a strong personal brand and stand out from the crowd. A well-crafted online presence can also help you communicate your unique qualities, making it easier for others to understand what you bring to the table.

Another important reason for building a personal online presence is to enhance your reputation. By sharing valuable content and engaging with others, you can establish yourself as an expert in your field and demonstrate your knowledge and skills. This can help you build a positive reputation, which can be especially important if you're looking to advance your career or grow your business. By establishing a positive online presence, you can demonstrate your commitment to your profession, your industry, and your personal brand.

Finally, building a personal online presence can help you connect with like-minded people and form new relationships. Social media platforms allow you to find people who share your interests, values, and experiences, and engage with them in a meaningful way. This can help you form new connections, collaborate with others, and find new opportunities. Whether you're looking to expand your network, find new business partners, or simply make new friends, having a strong online presence can be incredibly beneficial.

However, it is important to maintain control over one's online image and reputation, as sharing too much personal information online can lead to privacy concerns and online harassment. It is essential to be mindful of the information shared online and balance authenticity with adaptability.

Building a personal online presence is important for a variety of reasons. Whether you're looking to increase your visibility, build a personal brand, enhance your reputation, or connect with others, having a strong online presence can help you achieve your goals. So if you haven't already, now is the time to start building your personal online presence and take control of your online reputation.

Chapter 2

Defining Your Personal Brand

Personal branding is the process of creating a unique image or identity for yourself in the minds of others. It involves defining your values, skills, and personality traits, and then presenting them in a consistent and meaningful way to others. By developing a strong personal brand, you can differentiate yourself from others, communicate your value proposition, and achieve your professional and personal goals.

Defining your brand starts with self-reflection and self-discovery. This involves identifying your values, skills, and personality traits, as well as your passions and goals. Ask yourself what makes you unique and what you have to offer the world. What are your strengths, weaknesses, and areas for growth? Understanding these elements will help you define the essence of your brand.

Once you have a clear understanding of your personal brand, the next step is to communicate it effectively to others. This involves developing a personal brand statement, a clear and concise message that summarizes who you are and what you have to offer. Your personal brand statement should be unique to you and communicate your value proposition.

It is also important to be consistent in your personal branding efforts. This means that the way you present yourself online, in person, and in your professional interactions should align with your personal brand statement. This consistency helps to reinforce your brand and makes it easier for others to understand and remember who you are.

One way to build and maintain your personal brand is through social media. Social media provides a platform to showcase your personal brand, share your content and ideas, and connect with others. However, it is important to be mindful of the information shared on social media and to maintain control over your online image and reputation.

Another way to reinforce your personal brand is through networking and professional development. Attend events and conferences related to your industry, participate in professional organizations, and engage in ongoing learning and development activities. These opportunities allow you to connect with others, showcase your expertise, and reinforce your personal brand.

Defining your personal brand is a crucial aspect of personal growth and self-development. It involves self-reflection and self-discovery, communicating your brand effectively to others, and being consistent in your personal branding efforts. By developing a strong personal brand, you can differentiate yourself from others, communicate your value proposition, and achieve your professional and personal goals.

The importance of defining your personal brand

Defining your personal brand is important; as it helps you stand out in a crowded job market, establish credibility and expertise, and pursue your professional and personal goals with clarity and purpose. Here are some key benefits of defining your personal brand:

1. **Distinction:** Defining your personal brand helps you differentiate yourself from others, making you more memorable and distinctive in the eyes of potential employers, clients, and customers.
2. **Credibility:** A well-defined personal brand demonstrates your expertise and knowledge in your field, establishing credibility and trust with others.
3. **Career Advancement:** A strong personal brand can help you advance your career by attracting new opportunities, building a stronger professional network, and positioning yourself as a thought leader in your industry.
4. **Clarity of Purpose:** Defining your personal brand clarifies your goals and values, providing a clear sense of direction and purpose for your career and personal life.
5. **Confidence:** Having a well-defined personal brand can increase your confidence by helping you communicate your value proposition and presenting your unique skills and qualities in a consistent and meaningful way.

In conclusion, defining your personal brand is an important aspect of personal growth and development. It helps you stand out, establish credibility, pursue your goals with clarity and purpose, and build confidence in yourself and your abilities. By taking the time to define and communicate your personal brand, you can take control of your professional and personal future and achieve greater success and fulfillment.

Understanding your values, strengths, and unique qualities

Understanding one's values, strengths, and unique qualities is crucial for personal growth and success. Values are principles and beliefs that guide our decisions and actions. They help us determine what is important to us and what we stand for. Strengths are traits or skills that come naturally to us and that we excel at. Unique qualities are characteristics that set us apart from others and make us who we are.

Understanding your value

Understanding one's values is a crucial aspect of personal growth and well-being. Values are the principles and beliefs that guide our decisions and actions, and they help us determine what is important to us and what we stand for. Understanding your values can help you make informed decisions, set priorities, and live a more fulfilling life.

To understand your values, take the time to reflect on what you believe in and what motivates you. Consider what you prioritize in your life and what causes or activities you feel passionate about. Ask yourself what you value most and what you would be willing to stand up for. This self-reflection can help you identify your core values and give you a clear understanding of what matters to you.

You can also seek feedback from others to get a better understanding of your values. For example, you can ask friends and family members what they think you value most and what they believe are your core principles.

Once you have a clear understanding of your values, you can use this knowledge to make informed decisions about your personal and professional lives. For example, you can choose careers and hobbies that align with your values and ensure that your actions are in line with your beliefs. Understanding your values is a crucial part of personal growth and success. By reflecting on what matters to you and what you believe in, you can make informed decisions, set priorities, and live a more fulfilling life.

Understanding your strengths

Understanding one's strengths is an important aspect of personal growth and success. Strengths are traits or skills that come naturally to you and that you excel at. These can include things like creativity, problem-solving, communication, leadership, and organization, among others. To understand your strengths, take the time to reflect on your natural abilities and the things that you enjoy doing. Ask for feedback from others and consider the compliments you have received. Make a list of tasks and activities that you find easy and engaging, and think about what you excel at. This self-reflection can help you identify your unique talents and develop a clear understanding of your strengths.

Using your strengths can lead to increased self-confidence, motivation, and job satisfaction. When you are using your strengths, you are more likely to be engaged in your work and feel a sense of fulfillment. This, in turn, can lead to higher levels of productivity and success. On the other hand, when you are not using your strengths, you may feel unfulfilled, unmotivated, and less productive.

In addition to personal benefits, understanding your strengths can also help you make informed decisions about your career and personal life. By choosing careers and hobbies that align with your strengths, you can increase your chances of success and satisfaction. By reflecting on what you excel at and what comes naturally to you, you can make informed decisions, increase your self-confidence, and live a fulfilling life. So take the time to understand your strengths and use them to your advantage.

Understanding your unique qualities

Understanding one's unique qualities is essential for personal growth and success. Unique qualities are the characteristics that set an individual apart from others and make them who they are. To understand your unique qualities, take the time to reflect on what makes you different and special. Consider your personality traits, interests, experiences, and skills. Think about what you bring to the table that others cannot, and what sets you apart from others.

It is also helpful to ask for feedback from friends, family, and colleagues to gain a different perspective on your unique qualities. This can help you identify traits that you may have taken for granted or may not have even realized are unique to you.

Once you have a clear understanding of your unique qualities, you can use this knowledge to make informed decisions about your personal and professional life. For example, you can use your unique qualities to stand out in your chosen field and set yourself apart from others. You can also choose careers and hobbies that allow you to showcase your unique traits and abilities.

In conclusion, understanding your unique qualities is a crucial step in personal growth and success. By taking the time to reflect on what sets you apart and what makes you special, you can make informed decisions and live a fulfilling life. Embrace your unique qualities and use them to make a positive impact on the world.

Creating a personal mission statement

Understanding the Purpose of a Personal Mission Statement

A personal mission statement is a declaration of your purpose, goals, and values that defines who you are and what you stand for. It is a roadmap that guides you through life and helps you make decisions that align with your priorities and aspirations. Creating a personal mission statement is a powerful tool for personal growth and success, and it is a process that requires time, reflection, and introspection.

To create a personal mission statement, start by reflecting on your values, strengths, and unique qualities. Consider what you believe in, what you are passionate about, and what you want to achieve in life. Next, think about your short-term and long-term goals, and what you want to accomplish in your personal and professional lives.

Once you have a clear understanding of your values, goals, and aspirations, start to craft your personal mission statement. Keep it concise and to the point, and make sure it is easy to understand and remember. Your personal mission statement should articulate your purpose and be a true representation of who you are and what you stand for.

When writing your personal mission statement, consider using affirmations, such as "I am", "I will", or "I will strive to". This will make your statement more action-oriented and help you stay focused on your goals. Additionally, consider using language that is inspiring and motivating, and make sure your mission statement reflects your values and aspirations.

Once you have written your personal mission statement, read it regularly and use it as a guide for your decisions and actions. Consider sharing it with trusted friends or family members, and seeking their feedback and support. This can help you stay accountable and on track, and it can also provide you with valuable insights and perspectives.

It is important to note that a personal mission statement is not a static document, and may change over time as you grow and evolve. Be open to making changes to your mission statement as needed, and continue to reflect on your values, strengths, and unique qualities.

In conclusion, creating a personal mission statement is a powerful tool for personal growth and success. It helps you define your purpose, prioritize your goals, and align your decisions and actions with your values and aspirations. By taking the time to reflect on who you are and what you stand for, you can create a personal mission statement that will guide you through life and help you achieve your full potential.

Defining your core values

Defining your core values is an important step in creating a personal mission statement. Core values are the guiding principles that shape your beliefs and actions, and they serve as a foundation for your personal and professional life. Here are some steps for defining your core values:

1. **Reflect on Your Experiences:** Consider your past experiences and the things that have been important to you throughout your life. This can help you identify patterns and common themes that are relevant to your values.
2. **Identify Your Priorities:** Think about what you consider to be the most important things in your life, such as family, relationships, career, health, and personal growth.
3. **Create a List of Values:** Write down a list of values that align with your priorities and experiences. Some common values include honesty, integrity, responsibility, compassion, and respect.
4. **Narrow Your List:** Review your list and identify the values that are most important to you. Narrow your list to a smaller group of core values, typically between 5-7 values.
5. **Refine Your Values:** Once you have a list of core values, take the time to refine and clarify each value. For example, what does "honesty" mean to you and how does it impact your life?
6. **Test Your Values:** Consider how your core values apply to different aspects of your life, such as your relationships, career, and personal growth. This can help you determine if your values are truly reflective of who you are.

By defining your core values, you can gain a better understanding of what is truly important to you, and use this information to guide your decision-making and create a personal mission statement that truly represents who you are and what you stand for.

Tips on crafting a Personal Mission Statement:

1. **Start with self-reflection**: Identify your values, beliefs, and purpose in life. Ask yourself what you want to stand for and what legacy you want to leave.

2. **Keep it concise and clear:** A mission statement should be short, simple, and easy to remember. Avoid using complex language or abstract concepts.
3. **Make it inspiring and motivating:** Write a statement that energizes and drives you to achieve your goals. Use positive language and focus on the benefits of achieving your mission.
4. **Make it actionable:** Ensure your mission statement outlines specific, measurable, achievable, relevant, and time-bound (SMART) goals.
5. **Incorporate your values:** Your mission statement should reflect what you stand for, so make sure it aligns with your values and beliefs.
6. **Review and revise:** Your mission statement should evolve with you, so regularly review and revise it to ensure it remains relevant and inspiring.
7. **Share it with others:** Sharing your mission statement with friends, family, or colleagues can help keep you accountable and on track.

Examples of a Personal Mission Statement:

Example 1: "To live a fulfilling life by making a positive impact on others, continuously learning and growing, and pursuing my passions with integrity, creativity, and perseverance."

Example 2: "To be a source of inspiration and support to those around me, by living with kindness, empathy, and compassion, and constantly seeking self-improvement, knowledge, and growth. To use my skills and abilities to make a positive difference in the world, and leave a legacy of love, positivity, and impact."

Living Your Mission

Living your mission statement involves incorporating it into your daily life and using it as a guide for decision-making, setting goals, and taking action. A personal mission statement should not just be a piece of paper, but a living document that reflects your values, aspirations, and priorities. Here are some ways to make your mission statement an active part of your life:

1. **Use it as a decision-making tool:** Your mission statement should serve as a roadmap for your life, and it should help you make decisions that align with your values and goals. When faced with a difficult decision, consider how it fits with your mission statement and ask yourself if it is in line with your priorities and aspirations.
2. **Set goals based on your mission:** Your mission statement should inspire and guide your goals, both short-term and long-term. Consider setting goals that align with your mission statement and that support your values and aspirations. Make sure your goals are achievable, measurable, and specific.
3. **Take action:** Your mission statement should motivate and inspire you to take action towards your goals. Start by setting small, achievable goals, and take actionable steps to achieve them. Celebrate your successes, and use them as motivation to continue working towards your larger goals.
4. **Reflect regularly:** Regular reflection and introspection are key to living your mission statement. Take time to reflect on your values, strengths, and unique qualities, and assess how well you are living your mission. Consider making changes to your mission statement as needed, and continue to reflect on how it aligns with your life.
5. **Surround yourself with supportive people:** Surrounding yourself with supportive people who share your values and

aspirations can help you stay on track and achieve your goals. Consider seeking out a mentor, coach, or accountability partner who can support and encourage you in living your mission.

In conclusion, living your mission statement involves making it an active part of your life and using it as a guide for decision-making, setting goals, and taking action. By reflecting regularly, taking action, and surrounding yourself with supportive people, you can achieve your goals and live a fulfilling life that is in line with your values and aspirations.

Chapter 3

Building a personal online presence

Building a personal online presence is becoming increasingly important in today's digital world. It can help you establish your brand, connect with others, and advance your career or personal goals. Here are some steps for building a strong personal online presence:

1. **Choose Your Platforms**: There are many social media platforms available, each with its unique audience and purpose. Choose the platforms that align with your personal brand and goals, and focus your efforts on building a strong presence on those platforms.
2. **Define Your Brand:** Consider what you want your personal brand to be and what you want to be known for. This will help guide your content creation and interactions on social media.
3. **Create Quality Content:** Share content that aligns with your personal brand and goals, and focus on creating high-quality content that adds value to your followers. This can include blog posts, videos, photos, and more.
4. **Engage with Others:** Building a personal online presence is not just about creating content, it's also about engaging with others. This can include responding to comments, participating in discussions, and following influencers and thought leaders in your industry.
5. **Stay Consistent:** Maintaining a consistent personal brand across your social media platforms is important for building a strong personal online presence. This includes using the same profile picture and username across all platforms, and regularly posting content that aligns with your brand.

6. **Protect Your Privacy:** Be mindful of the information you share online and take steps to protect your privacy. This includes being cautious about sharing personal information and adjusting your privacy settings on social media platforms to control who can see your content.

By following these steps, you can build a strong personal online presence that supports your personal brand and goals, and helps you connect with others in your industry or community.

Understanding the role of social media in personal branding

Social media has revolutionized the way individuals and businesses present themselves to the world. Personal branding refers to the practice of creating and promoting a unique image or identity in the market, and social media has made it easier than ever to establish and maintain a personal brand. In the following paragraphs, we will explore the role of social media in personal branding and its impact.

Social media provides a platform for individuals to showcase their skills, interests, and experiences to a global audience. This enables individuals to create and curate content that aligns with their personal brand, showcasing their unique value proposition to potential employers, customers, and partners. Platforms such as *LinkedIn, Twitter,* and *Instagram* allow individuals to network and connect with others in their industry, increasing their visibility and expanding their professional circle.

In addition, social media provides individuals with the ability to manage their online reputation, which is crucial to personal branding. Negative comments or incorrect information can quickly spread online, damaging a person's reputation. On the other hand, regularly posting positive and relevant content can enhance a person's brand and online reputation.

However, it is important to note that social media also presents certain challenges for personal branding. The abundance of content available online can make it difficult for individuals to stand out, and it can be difficult to maintain a consistent brand image across multiple platforms. Additionally, the ease of posting content on social media can also lead to individuals oversharing personal information, which can detract from their professional image.

In conclusion, social media plays a crucial role in personal branding, providing individuals with the ability to showcase their skills, interests, and experiences to a global audience. However, it is important to use social media strategically and maintain a consistent brand image to effectively enhance one's personal brand.

Choosing the right social media platforms for your personal brand

With so many social media platforms available, it can be challenging to determine which ones are right for your personal brand. It is important to choose platforms that align with your personal brand and target audience, allowing you to effectively showcase your skills, interests, and experiences to the world. To choose the right social media platforms for your personal brand, you need to consider the following.

- ➢ **Understanding Your Audience:** First, consider your target audience. Who you are trying to reach with your personal brand and where they are most likely to be active on social media. Depending on your target audience, certain platforms may be more effective than others. For example, if your target audience is primarily composed of professionals, *LinkedIn* may be the best platform to use, while if your target audience is interested in visual content, *Instagram* or *Pinterest* may be a better fit. This will help you determine which platforms are best suited for your personal brand.
- ➢ **Identifying Your Goals:** Determine what you want to achieve with your personal brand such as building your network, sharing your work, or promoting a cause. Depending on your goals, certain platforms may be more effective than others. For example, if your goal is to increase your visibility and reach a wider audience, platforms with a large user base, such as *Facebook* or *Twitter*, may be more suitable, while if your goal is to build a community around a particular topic, platforms like *Reddit* or *Quora* may be a better fit. This will help you choose platforms that align with your goals.
- ➢ **Evaluating Platform Features:** When evaluating platform features, it's crucial to consider the goals and objectives of your personal brand. Research the different features and capabilities of each platform, and consider

which ones are most important for your personal brand. Some platforms are better suited for sharing visual content, while others are better for writing-based content. For example, if visual content is a key component of your brand, platforms like *Instagram* or *Pinterest* may be a better fit, while platforms like *Medium* or *LinkedIn* may be better suited for writing-based content. Additionally, consider factors such as the ability to schedule posts, track analytics, and run ads. By selecting platforms that offer the features most important to your personal brand, you can maximize your reach and effectively communicate your message to your audience.

➢ **Assessing User Engagement:** Consider the level of engagement and interaction that is typical on each platform, and choose platforms that allow for meaningful engagement with your audience. To assess user engagement, it's important to understand the type of interaction that is typical on each platform and choose those that best fit your audience and goals. The level of engagement varies between platforms, with some being more suited to passive consumption (e.g. *Instagram, YouTube*) and others encouraging more active engagement through comments, likes, and shares (e.g. *Twitter, Facebook*). It's also important to consider the features each platform offers to facilitate interaction, such as polls, Q&A sessions, and live streams. By selecting platforms that allow for meaningful engagement with your audience, you can build a strong relationship with them and increase their loyalty to your brand.

> **Monitoring Your Results:** Once you have established your presence on a few platforms, track your results and adjust your strategy as needed. This can include monitoring your engagement levels, traffic, and other key metrics to determine which platforms are working best for you and your personal brand.

It is important to remember that social media is constantly evolving, and it is important to keep up with the latest trends and changes. What works for one person may not work for another and it is important to experiment and be open to trying new platforms. Additionally, it is important to be consistent and maintain a consistent brand image across all platforms to effectively enhance your personal brand.

By carefully selecting the right social media platforms for your personal brand, you can maximize your reach and engagement, and build a strong online presence that supports your goals and personal brand.

Developing a strong online presence through content creation

Developing a strong online presence through content creation is essential for building a personal brand, connecting with your audience, and growing your network. With so many platforms and channels available, it's important to understand the importance of content creation and how to leverage it effectively.

One of the first steps in developing a strong online presence is to define your target audience and understand their needs, interests, and preferences. This will help you create content that resonates with them and encourages engagement.

Once you have a clear understanding of your audience, it's time to start creating content. The type of content you create will depend on your personal brand and the platforms you are using. For example, if your personal brand focuses on visual content, platforms like *Instagram* and *Pinterest* may be a better fit, while if your brand focuses on writing, platforms like *Medium* or *LinkedIn* may be a better choice.

When creating content, it's important to focus on quality over quantity. Create content that is relevant, engaging, and adds value to your audience. This can include blog posts, videos, podcasts, and info graphics, among others. Make sure to use high-quality images and engaging visuals to help your content stand out.

In addition to creating content, it's also important to share it with your network and engage with your audience. Respond to comments and feedback, participate in online conversations, and share your content on other relevant platforms and channels. This will help you build a strong following and increase your reach.

It's also important to track your content's performance and measure its success. Use analytics tools to monitor your reach, engagement, and overall performance. This will help you identify what's working and what's not, and make informed decisions about future content creation.

Finally, consistency is key to developing a strong online presence.

Consistently create and share high-quality content that aligns with your personal brand and resonates with your audience. This will help you establish yourself as a thought leader in your industry and build a loyal following.

Developing a strong online presence through content creation is an essential component of building a personal brand and connecting with your audience. By understanding your target audience, creating quality content, engaging with your network, and consistently sharing your content, you can build a strong online presence and reach your goals.

Optimizing your online profiles for search engines

Optimizing your online profiles for search engines is essential for improving your visibility and attracting new followers and potential customers. Search engines use complex algorithms to determine the relevance and ranking of search results, and having a well-optimized online profile can help you rank higher and reach a wider audience. Here are some tips to help you optimize your online profiles for search engines:

Choose the right keywords: Keywords are the words and phrases that describe your personal brand, products, or services. Choose keywords that accurately reflect your personal brand and target audience, and include them in your profile, bio, and content.

Use a consistent name and handle: Using a consistent name and handle across all of your online profiles can help search engines better understand and associate your online presence. Choose a handle that accurately reflects your personal brand and is easy to remember.

Create a comprehensive profile: A comprehensive profile can help you stand out from the crowd and attract more followers. Include a professional profile picture, a detailed bio that describes your personal brand and experience, and any relevant links to your website or other social media profiles.

Post regularly: Regular posting is essential for keeping your profile active and engaging with your audience. The frequency of your posts will depend on your personal brand and target audience, but aim to post regularly and consistently to keep your profile up-to-date and relevant.

Engage with your audience: Engaging with your audience is essential for building a strong online presence and improving your search engine ranking. Respond to comments, participate in online conversations, and share other relevant content to build a strong following and increase your reach.

Use tags and hashtags: Using tags and hashtags can help you reach a wider audience and improve your search engine ranking. Choose relevant tags and hashtags that accurately reflect your personal brand and target audience, and include them in your posts and updates.

Monitor and improve your performance: Use analytics tools to monitor your performance and identify areas for improvement. Use this information to make informed decisions about your online presence and adjust your strategy accordingly.

In conclusion, optimizing your online profiles for search engines is essential for improving your visibility, building a strong online presence, and attracting new followers and potential customers. By using the right keywords, creating a comprehensive profile, posting regularly, engaging with your audience, using tags and hashtags, and monitoring and improving your performance, you can optimize your online profiles for search engines and reach your goals.

Chapter 4

Networking and building relationships

Networking and building relationships is a crucial aspect of personal growth and self development. Attend events, utilize social media and professional networking sites, offer help and support, follow up with new connections, cultivate relationships, and be authentic. These actions help build a supportive community and advance your career goals.

Here are some tips for building and maintaining relationships:

Attend Networking Events: Attend events and conferences related to your industry or interests to meet new people and build your network. This can include local networking events, online meetups, and industry-specific conferences.

Connect Online: Utilize social media platforms and professional networking sites such as LinkedIn to connect with others in your industry or community.

Offer Help and Support: Build relationships by offering help and support to others. This can include providing valuable information, sharing your expertise, or simply being a supportive friend.

Follow Up: After meeting someone new, be sure to follow up with them to maintain the connection. This can include sending an email, connecting on social media, or meeting for coffee or lunch.

Cultivate Relationships: Relationships take time and effort to build and maintain. Make an effort to regularly check in with your connections, and offer help and support when needed.

Be Authentic: Building strong relationships requires authenticity. Be yourself, and let your personality shine through in your interactions with others.

Networking and building relationships can help you advance your career, build a supportive community, and achieve your personal goals. By following these tips, you can develop strong, meaningful relationships that support your personal growth and self development.

The power of networking in personal branding

Networking is a powerful tool for building and promoting your personal brand. By connecting with others in your industry or community, you can expand your reach, establish yourself as a thought leader, and build relationships that can support your personal and professional goals.

One of the key benefits of networking is the ability to build relationships and expand your network. By connecting with others, you can meet potential collaborators, partners, mentors, and friends who can offer support and guidance as you grow and develop. Networking can also help you build your reputation and establish yourself as a thought leader in your industry or community. When you regularly engage with others, share your ideas, and demonstrate your expertise, others will come to know you as a valuable resource and thought leader.

Networking can also help you stay current and up-to-date on the latest trends and developments in your industry or community. By attending events and engaging with others, you can stay informed about the latest developments and stay ahead of the curve. This can give you a competitive edge and help you establish yourself as a leading voice in your field.

Another benefit of networking is the opportunity to promote your personal brand and reach a wider audience. When you engage with others, share your ideas, and build relationships, you can increase your visibility and reach a wider audience. This can help you promote your personal brand, and increase your chances of finding new opportunities and advancing your career.

Networking can be a valuable source of inspiration and motivation. When you connect with others who share your interests and passions, you can gain a new perspective and find inspiration to pursue your goals. This can help you stay motivated and focused, and can help you achieve your personal and professional goals more effectively.

In conclusion, the power of networking in personal branding is undeniable. By connecting with others, building relationships, and sharing your ideas, you can establish yourself as a thought leader, expand your reach, and promote your personal brand. By making networking a priority, you can take your personal brand to the next level and achieve your personal and professional goals.

Building relationships through social media

Building relationships through social media is a crucial aspect of personal growth and self development in today's digital age. With billions of active users on various social media platforms, the opportunities to connect and build relationships with others are endless. Whether you are looking to promote your personal brand, expand your network, or advance your career, social media provides a wealth of opportunities to connect with others and build meaningful relationships.

One of the key benefits of using social media to build relationships is the ability to reach a wider audience. By leveraging the power of social media, you can expand your reach and connect with people from all over the world. This can help you build a diverse network of contacts, and can increase your chances of finding new opportunities and advancing your career.

Another benefit of using social media to build relationships is the ability to connect with like-minded individuals. By engaging with others in your industry or community, you can find others who share your interests, passions, and goals. This can help you build strong, supportive relationships, and can provide you with a source of inspiration and motivation as you pursue your goals.

In addition to connecting with others, social media also provides a platform for building your personal brand. By creating a strong online presence, you can establish yourself as a thought leader in your industry or community, and promote your expertise and skills. Whether you are sharing your thoughts, ideas, or projects, social media provides a powerful tool for promoting your personal brand and reaching a wider audience.

Another benefit of using social media to build relationships is the ability to stay current and up-to-date on the latest trends and developments. By following others in your industry or community, you can stay informed about the latest news, trends, and developments, and stay ahead of the curve. This can give you a competitive edge, and can help you establish yourself as a leading voice in your field.

Finally, social media provides a platform for building relationships and fostering community. By engaging with others, sharing your ideas, and participating in online discussions, you can build a supportive network of friends and colleagues who can offer support and guidance as you pursue your goals. Whether you are looking to advance your career, build your personal brand, or just connect with like-minded individuals, social media provides a powerful tool for building relationships and fostering community.

In conclusion, building relationships through social media is a crucial aspect of personal growth and self development in today's digital age. By leveraging the power of social media, you can connect with others, build your personal brand, stay informed about the latest trends and developments, and build a supportive network of friends and colleagues. Whether you are looking to advance your career, build your personal brand, or just connect with like-minded individuals, social media provides a powerful tool for building relationships and fostering community.

Developing strong communication skills

Developing strong communication skills is essential for success in personal and professional life. Effective communication involves more than just speaking; it also encompasses listening, writing, and nonverbal cues. Here are some tips for developing strong communication skills.

Listen actively: Active listening involves paying attention to the speaker, understanding their perspective, and providing feedback. This involves being present in the moment, avoiding distractions, and asking clarifying questions when necessary.

Practice clear and concise speaking: Speak in a clear, concise manner, using simple language and avoiding complex jargon. This will help ensure that your message is understood by your audience.

Write clearly and effectively: Writing is an important aspect of communication, and it is important to develop strong writing skills. This includes using clear and concise language, avoiding spelling and grammar errors, and using appropriate formatting.

Pay attention to nonverbal cues: Nonverbal cues such as body language, tone of voice, and eye contact can greatly impact how your message is received. It is important to be aware of your own nonverbal cues, as well as those of others, to effectively communicate and understand others.

Be adaptable: Communication is a dynamic process, and it is important to be able to adjust your communication style based on the audience and situation. For example, communication in a professional setting may be more formal, while communication in a personal setting may be more casual.

Seek feedback: Feedback is an important aspect of communication, and it is important to regularly seek feedback from others on your communication skills. This can help you identify areas for improvement and make necessary adjustments.

Practice: Communication skills can be improved through regular practice. Participate in public speaking opportunities, join a debate club, or engage in discussions with friends and family. The more you practice, the more confident and effective you will become.

In conclusion, strong communication skills are essential for success in personal and professional life. By actively listening, speaking clearly and concisely, writing effectively, paying attention to nonverbal cues, being adaptable, seeking feedback, and practicing regularly, you can develop strong communication skills that will serve you well in all areas of life.

Chapter 5

Balancing authenticity and adaptability

Balancing authenticity and adaptability is an essential part aspect of personal and professional growth. Authenticity refers to being true to oneself and one's values, beliefs, and personality, while adaptability refers to the ability to change and adjust to different circumstances and environments. In today's rapidly changing world, both authenticity and adaptability are necessary for success, but finding the right balance between them can be challenging.

On one hand, being authentic is crucial for maintaining one's identity and self-esteem. When people are authentic, they are confident in who they are and what they believe in. This sense of self allows them to communicate effectively with others and form meaningful relationships. Moreover, authenticity can also lead to a sense of purpose and fulfillment as individuals can align their actions with their values and beliefs.

On the other hand, adaptability is essential for survival and success in today's dynamic environment. The ability to change and adjust to new circumstances and situations is crucial for personal and professional growth. By being adaptable, individuals can learn new skills, embrace new ideas, and respond to new challenges. Moreover, adaptability can also lead to personal growth and improvement, as individuals can learn from their experiences and apply new insights to their lives.

However, finding the right balance between authenticity and adaptability can be challenging. Being too authentic can lead to a lack of flexibility and a rigid mindset, which can prevent individuals from adapting to new circumstances and situations. On the other hand, being too adaptable can lead to a loss of identity and self-esteem, as individuals may struggle to maintain their values and beliefs in the face of new challenges.

To find the right balance between authenticity and adaptability, it is important to understand that both are important, but they must be balanced in different ways depending on the situation. In some situations, being authentic may be more important, while in others, adaptability may be more crucial. For example, in a professional setting, it may be important to adapt to the expectations and norms of the workplace, while still being true to one's values and beliefs.

It is also important to be self-aware and reflect on one's values, beliefs, and personality. By understanding themselves, individuals can identify the situations where authenticity or adaptability are more important, and adjust their behavior accordingly. Moreover, self-awareness can also help individuals understand their limitations and areas where they can improve.

In conclusion, balancing authenticity and adaptability is a critical aspect of personal and professional growth. Both are important for success, but finding the right balance between them can be challenging. To find the right balance, it is important to understand the situation and be self-aware. By being authentic and adaptable, individuals can communicate effectively with others, form meaningful relationships, and grow professionally and personally.

Balancing Authenticity with Adaptability

Here are some tips to help you balance authenticity with adaptability:

1. **Know your audience:** Understanding your target audience and their needs, interests, and preferences is essential for balancing authenticity with adaptability. This will help you create content that resonates with them and aligns with your personal brand.
2. **Be clear about your values:** Define your values and what is important to you. This will help you stay true to your personal brand and remain authentic, even as you adapt and evolve.
3. **Be open to feedback:** Engage with your audience and be open to feedback and constructive criticism. This will help you understand what is working and what is not, and make informed decisions about adapting your brand.
4. **Experiment with new content formats**: Experimenting with new content formats, such as videos, podcasts, or infographics, can help you stay relevant and engage with your audience. However, make sure that the new formats align with your personal brand and values.
5. **Stay up-to-date with industry trends:** Staying up-to-date with industry trends and developments can help you remain relevant and competitive. However, it's important to be selective about which trends you adopt and make sure that they align with your personal brand.
6. **Maintain a consistent voice and tone**: Maintaining a consistent voice and tone is essential for building a strong personal brand and establishing credibility. Be mindful of

the language and tone you use in your posts, updates, and interactions with your audience.
7. **Be yourself:** Above all, it's important to be yourself and stay true to your personal brand. Don't try to be someone you're not or adopt a persona that doesn't align with your values and beliefs.

In conclusion, balancing authenticity with adaptability is a crucial aspect of building a personal brand and achieving success online. By understanding your target audience, defining your values, being open to feedback, experimenting with new content formats, staying up-to-date with industry trends, maintaining a consistent voice and tone, and being yourself, you can balance authenticity with adaptability and reach your goals.

Importance of being authentic in personal branding

Being authentic is crucial for personal branding, as it helps individuals establish their unique identity and stand out in a crowded market. Personal branding is about creating a consistent image of oneself and communicating it effectively to others. Authenticity is the foundation of this process, as it ensures that the image that is being communicated is true to who the individual is and what they stand for.

An authentic personal brand is more likely to be memorable and impactful, as it is based on genuine qualities and experiences. Authenticity also helps individuals build trust with their audience, as people can sense when someone is being genuine. A personal brand built on authenticity is more likely to attract the right opportunities and connect with the right people, as it is aligned with one's values and beliefs.

Moreover, being authentic helps individuals stay true to themselves and maintain their self-esteem. In a world where people are constantly trying to fit in and conform to expectations, being authentic can be a source of strength and resilience. When individuals are authentic, they are confident in who they are and what they stand for, which allows them to communicate effectively with others and form meaningful relationships.

However, being authentic in personal branding requires self-awareness and reflection. Individuals need to understand their values, beliefs, and personality to communicate their brand effectively. It also requires a willingness to be vulnerable and share one's story, even if it is not always easy or popular.

Navigating different online and in-person environments

Navigating different online and in-person environments can be challenging, as each environment has its unique norms, customs, and expectations. To be successful and effective, it is important to understand and adapt to these different environments.

For online environments, such as social media and virtual meeting platforms, it is important to be mindful of the tone and language you use. Consider using more formal language, as online communication can often be misinterpreted, and avoid using emoticons or informal language that may not be appropriate in a professional setting. Additionally, be mindful of the information you share online and avoid sharing sensitive or confidential information.

In virtual meeting environments, it is important to be present and engaged, just as you would be in an in-person meeting. Arrive on time, dress appropriately, and make sure your background is professional and appropriate. Consider using a webcam and good lighting to enhance your presence, and be mindful of your body language and tone.

For in-person environments, it is important to understand the social norms and customs of the specific environment. For example, in a business setting, it is important to be professional and dressed appropriately and to use appropriate language and body language. In a social setting, it may be more relaxed and informal, but it is still important to be respectful and mindful of others.

In both online and in-person environments, it is important to be respectful and considerate of others. This includes being aware of cultural differences and being open to diversity, as well as avoiding insensitive or offensive language or behavior. Additionally, it is important to be an active listener and to be mindful of your communication style as well as the communication styles of others.

Navigating different online and in-person environments requires understanding and adapting to the unique norms, customs, and expectations of each environment. By being mindful of tone, language, and communication styles, as well as being respectful and considerate of others, you can effectively navigate and succeed in any environment.

Conclusion

In today's digital age, creating a memorable online presence and building your brand involves being intentional and strategic in the way you present yourself online.

One of the key components of creating a memorable online presence is having a professional profile picture and header image, as well as a clear and concise profile description. It is also important to be consistent in your use of language, tone, and content across all your social media platforms.

Building your brand involves creating content that aligns with your values, goals, and interests, and sharing it on relevant platforms. This could be in the form of blog posts, videos, podcasts, or social media updates. It is essential to be authentic and genuine in your content and to engage with your followers and other users on the platforms you use.

Networking is also a crucial aspect of building your online brand. By reaching out to other professionals and building relationships, you can increase your visibility, expand your reach, and build a supportive community.

Finally, it is important to regularly review and evaluate your online presence and to make changes and updates as needed. This can include updating your profile picture and bio, adjusting the content you share, and identifying areas where you can improve your online presence.

In conclusion, the virtual you is an essential aspect of personal and professional life in today's digital age. By being intentional and strategic in the way you present yourself online, creating content that aligns with your values, goals, and interests, networking with other professionals, and regularly evaluating your online presence, you can create a memorable online presence and build a strong brand.

www.ingramcontent.com/pod-product-compliance
Lightning Source LLC
Chambersburg PA
CBHW070321220526
45465CB00013B/2028